Safe at Last

True Stories of Horse Rescues

by
Elaine Pease

Photographs by
Roxanne Capaul

FILTER PRESS, LLC

Juvenile literature–Horses
Ages 7 and up

Acknowledgments

For their invaluable help, I wish to thank my friends at Colorado Horse Rescue: Carol Brice, Shawna English, Rachel Corbman, and Jenny Logan. To Debra Thomas at Horses Mending Hearts, Jackie Ashley at Wild at Heart and Sara Hughes Pease, thank you for helping me understand the important work of horse therapy. I thank Dana Pease for an educator's viewpoint on text and story. Thank you to Chad Bice, Sierra's dad and Poncho's owner; and Mark Gookin, Ringo's owner, for sharing details of their rescue stories. I'm so fortunate to have my supportive friends and colleagues in the Boulder Children's Writers Critique Group. They read this manuscript countless times and helped me polish it until it was ready to submit to my publisher. Then Doris Baker, my editor at Filter Press, made this book a wonderful reality. Thank you, all. As always, I'm grateful to my family, especially my husband, for their wise suggestions and understanding when dinner had to wait because of "one last edit."

ISBN: 978-0-86541-187-6
Library of Congress Control Number: 2015950414
Text copyright © 2015 Elaine Pease. All rights reserved.
Photographs copyright © Roxanne Capaul. Other photographs reprinted courtesy of
Colorado Horse Rescue, Sarah Hofkamp, Chad Bice, and Marc Gookin.

Cover and interior design by Roxanne Capaul.

Published by Filter Press, LLC, Palmer Lake, Colorado

Printed in the United States of America

CONTENTS

If this book can help make a difference in one child's
life, one horse's life, then it's served its purpose.
-Elaine Pease

Education and compassion are powerful elements
in the effort to help the disadvantaged horse.
-Roxanne Capaul

The morning sun peeks above the Colorado plains. Hawks and rabbits wake up. So do the hungry horses. At a special place called Colorado Horse Rescue, a **volunteer** drives a truck loaded with hay across the dirt pasture. Horses chase after the truck, eager for their breakfast. Another volunteer rides in the back and tosses hay to them. Fifty horses, ponies, and mules start munching on their meals. Many of them had been starving and near death before they were brought to the horse rescue.

A golf cart buzzes out of the barn toward the first pasture. The cart carries buckets of grain mixed with medicine. Each bucket is labeled with a horse's name. That way, the horses get the correct feed and medicine.

It does not matter if there is a snowstorm outside or if it is firecracker-hot. The workers at the horse rescue pull on their big boots and heavy gloves every day and get to work. They **muck** the stalls and pastures, even when the manure is frozen to the ground. They cool down overheated horses with sponge baths. They put medicine on horses' wounds. The hard work pays off when they see a horse is healing or—even better—is **adopted** into a loving family.

The amazing horses and volunteers at Colorado Horse Rescue inspired these six true stories.

3

PONCHO

Poncho

Hero

& HERO

Chapter 1

Poncho used to work as a trail horse at a dude ranch. The rest of the time, he was alone in his pen. Horses need a companion or to belong to a herd. They feel safer that way.

Someone noticed the skinny, lonely horse and called Animal Control. Workers from the horse rescue and an Animal Control officer hiked up an icy mountain road. They waited at the meeting spot for the ranch owner. He finally appeared, leading Poncho. Poncho's dull golden coat barely stretched over his ribs. Ticks crawled over his body. His hooves were so long they had curled up.

The Animal Control officer could have forced the owner to give up Poncho. (That is called forced surrender.) Instead, the officer used kind words. She knew that the owner could not afford to care for Poncho. The officer explained it was better for Poncho and the owner to surrender the horse. Kind words often work better than forcing someone to give up their animal.

The rescue team led the **scruffy** horse down the road. They loaded Poncho into a trailer and drove him to his new home at the horse rescue.

Little did Poncho know that he would soon have a friend. An eight-year-old girl named Sierra visited the horse rescue often. She was especially fond of a sweet, blind horse named Jesse. One day, when Sierra arrived to see Jesse, he was not in the pasture. Her favorite horse had been adopted.

A new horse had filled Jesse's spot—Poncho. Something about him made Sierra think he needed a friend. Poncho turned his head and noticed Sierra, and they walked toward each other. Sierra reached through the fence and stroked Poncho's neck.

Poncho

Jesse

This was the horse she had been waiting for. How could she earn enough money to adopt him? The adoption fee could cost $600 or more. She decided to do extra chores and save her birthday money. Earning enough money to adopt Poncho would take a long time. Sierra was determined to adopt her horse. Meanwhile, she would visit him as often as possible.

On one visit, a volunteer gave Sierra some bad news. A horse had kicked Poncho. The veterinarian at the horse rescue said that no one should ride Poncho. The injury was so bad that Poncho might never be ridden again.

Her dad asked, "Sierra, do you still want to adopt a horse that you can't ride?"

"Of course," Sierra replied. "Poncho is my horse."

Sierra and Poncho

Poncho healed at the horse rescue. Sierra never stopped visiting and comforting him. She continued to work and save money. Halloween arrived, but Sierra decided not to trick-or-treat for candy. She made a donation box instead. She went door-to-door with her parents and collected coins. The money was for the horse rescue and for Poncho's medical care. Sierra loved candy, but she loved Poncho more!

A horse named Hero joined Poncho in his pen. Hero was very ill and weak. The two became good friends, which seemed to help them get better. If they were more than ten feet apart, they whinnied to each other. The farther apart they were, the louder they whinnied. The two horses even looked alike. The white **blaze** on Poncho's nose curved to the right. Hero's blaze curved to the left. Poncho's right legs had white **stockings**. Hero's stockings were on his left legs.

Poncho, Sierra, and Hero

A family adopted Hero and moved him to their home. Hero became sick again, so sick that he almost died. His new owners made a tough decision. They returned him to the horse rescue. As soon as Hero was alongside Poncho, his health improved. Poncho's leg had mended, too. He could be ridden again!

A year had passed since Sierra met Poncho. She had saved all her money. With her parents' help, she adopted her dream horse.

Poncho and Hero missed each other. Poncho's head drooped and his eyes had lost their sparkle. Sierra and her parents heard that Hero acted the same way. Clearly, the two horses were meant to be forever friends. Sierra's family decided to adopt Hero as well.

Poncho and Hero now stand side-by-side in a warm barn and run in a pasture together. The love of one determined little girl made it possible.

Poncho is a Palomino breed. Palominos are known for their golden coats with blond manes and tails. A breed is a type of horse. There are more than 250 horse breeds worldwide. Hero is an American Quarter Horse breed. The Quarter Horse is the most popular breed in America. The breed got its name by winning quarter-mile races held on the main streets of towns. Quarter Horses can run up to 55 mph! (That is the speed limit for cars on many highways.)

Mini Pearl is Colorado Horse Rescue's Ambassador. She tells you horse facts straight from the Mini's mouth.

Topaz

TOPAZ

Chapter 2

The rescue horses **whinny** to the golf cart as it arrives with their grain buckets. The horses want their food now! When Topaz first arrived at the rescue, she never whinnied for her meals. The skinny Paint horse kept still and quiet. She was badly **malnourished**. Even so, she did not paw the ground when breakfast arrived, like the other horses. Topaz had learned patience the hard way.

Before they were rescued, Topaz and her horse companions stood in a tiny corral in the mountains day after day. Their owner never let the horses out for exercise. They were seldom fed. The horses **scrounged** through the dust in the corral for anything to eat.

The owner decided to surrender the horses to the rescue. A veterinarian examined Topaz and found her belly filled with sand and dirt. The workers treated all the horses, but Topaz was the most ill. She could barely eat. The veterinarian inserted a tube through her nose into her stomach. For three days, the workers gave her medicine through the tube to keep Topaz alive.

On the fourth morning, the mare was perky and hungry for breakfast. Hooray! The medicine worked. She gobbled every bit of grain and alfalfa at each feeding.

Topaz gained more than 100 pounds. Soon she was back to her normal weight of 1,200 pounds. A worker noticed her gentle spirit and thought she would make a perfect **therapy** horse.

Topaz got a job helping people with physical and emotional **disabilities**. Children who use wheelchairs can learn how it feels to walk when they ride Topaz. Teenagers may have trouble at school or making friends, but they feel happier and safe with Topaz. Sometimes all a person needs is a friend. Topaz is that friend.

Topaz is a Paint mare. A mare is a female horse. Paint horses have coats with splashes of white and either brown, black, or gray. The Plains Indians tamed the breed because these horses are strong and brave.

Horse Therapy

Horse therapy can help heal people's minds and bodies. A person who attends a horse therapy program is paired with a horse chosen especially for him or her. The horses are often adopted from a **rescue facility**. A therapy horse must be gentle and patient, like Topaz. Riders learn how to be calm, brave, and responsible. Therapy horses are good teachers, because they are experts at overcoming bad experiences. Horse therapy can aid people who are injured or disabled. Riders feel the horse's movement. This helps the rider's muscles to work better.

Ringo

RINGO

Chapter 3

Children rode Ringo at a summer camp for more than twenty years. Then Ringo became sick and could not be ridden. He had bad teeth, too, because no one had taken care of them. Like humans, horses need to have their teeth checked. Ringo's teeth were in such poor shape that it hurt to chew. He could not eat enough food to stay healthy, and he lost a lot of weight.

A kind person brought Ringo to the horse rescue facility. Ringo grew stronger with medicine and care. The volunteers softened his food in water. He made lots of friends among the volunteers and horses. Ringo always galloped to the gate to greet a new horse when it arrived.

Still shaggy and thin, Ringo was not the most handsome horse at the rescue. A family stopped by, looking for a horse to foster. They did not care about Ringo's looks and fell in love with him anyway.

Ringo was released into his new pasture at his foster home. He did not fit into the herd right away. He stood apart from the other horses and hung his head. Members of the herd picked on him with nips and kicks. After a while, Ringo seemed to have had enough. He kicked back. That was enough to make the other horses stop bullying him. The herd now respects him, and Ringo holds his head high.

Ringo is a Palomino gelding. A gelding is a male horse that cannot produce **offspring**. Stallions are male horses that can produce offspring. In a herd, the stallion is not the leader. A mare actually leads the herd and alerts the others to danger. The female leader is called the "boss mare."

Ringo and his new herd

Fostering & Sponsoring

Besides adoption, another way to help a rescue horse is to be a foster family. A fostered horse is cared for until another family can adopt it. People who do not have a barn can sponsor a horse at a rescue facility. They choose a horse to sponsor and donate money every month for its feed and care.

BABY JINI

& ANGEL

Chapter 4

Two-week-old Jini was barely alive. Her mom, Angel, and six other Mustangs were in the same condition. The horses lived on a Nebraska ranch in a crowded pen. They had no food or clean water. Other Mustangs in the pen had died.

The sheriff's department and the Humane Society closed down the ranch. The Humane Society fed and watered the horses and contacted the horse rescue to come save the Mustangs before more died. A rescue team drove for eight hours from Colorado to Nebraska.

To ready them for the long journey, the workers gave the horses more food and water. Eight terrified Mustangs were loaded into a horse trailer and driven through the night back to Colorado.

No one knew if the horses would survive the trip.

The morning was still dark when they pulled into the horse rescue. The tired workers unloaded the horses from the trailer. Angel was close to dying, but she kept Jini alive by **nursing** her.

Over the next weeks, the volunteers tended to Angel and the other Mustangs. The horses soon reached a healthy weight. Jini grew into a beautiful and smart horse. One of the workers realized Jini was special and adopted her.

Jini and her owner now work together at a therapy program that helps people with special needs. Sometimes people who need therapy meet inside a hospital or at a doctor's office. Jini's special friends meet in a barn.

The large barn does not look at all like a doctor's office, or smell like one, either. The air is filled with the smell of horse manure and sawdust. Birds fly through the barn door and overhead. The people, who have come for help, enjoy the different sights and scents and being around animals.

Mustangs

The Mustang breed is small and **hardy**. Spanish explorers brought Mustangs to the American Plains from Spain, more than 400 years ago. The word Mustang is from the Spanish word *mustengo*. It means "ownerless beast" or "stray horse." Mustangs still run wild in western states.

Instead of riding Jini, they talk to her, groom her, or simply watch how she behaves.

When it is time to leave, everyone forms a circle around Jini. They all laugh when Jini carries her feed bowl in her teeth and places the bowl in her cubby. Jini shakes hands (hooves, really) with someone in the group and bows. She will be waiting for them when they return.

One person in the program said, "Jini shows me that if she can do these things, then I can do anything."

Jini had a rough start in life. She is a shining example of how life can get better.

Horses have their own special ways of communicating. They can swivel their ears. Ears pointing forward show other horses directions. Ears laid back signal a warning or fear. Horses "talk" using their eyes and swishing their tails, too. They also communicate by making sounds and even by breathing in different ways. Humans understand only a small part of how horses communicate with each other.

Jini

Cali and Knee-Hi

KNEE-HI

Chapter 5

Knee-Hi's name fits him well. He is twenty-four inches from hoof to ear! Knee-Hi's owners had tried to sell him when he was only three months old and too young to leave his mom. To keep them together, a horse rescue volunteer bought the baby Miniature horse and his mama. She could not afford to take care of the Minis and brought them to the rescue to live.

The colt and mother jumped around wildly as they were unloaded from the trailer. The volunteers made them feel at home with pats on the neck and soft words. In no time, Knee-Hi was galloping and kicking up his heels. Volunteers gave him a ball that was twice his size. Knee-Hi spent hours playing with it in the arena. One of Knee-Hi's human friends made a video of him with his ball. Search "Knee-Hi The Mighty Mini" to watch the funny video online.

Soon the colt grew old enough to leave his mom. A caring family adopted Knee-Hi and three other rescue horses. The family said, "We have a loving little herd of horses that most people have given up on. They are our angels in fur."

In 2006, the Guinness Book of World Records listed Thumbelina as the smallest Miniature horse. She was 17 1/2 inches tall! Most Minis measure 34 to 38 inches tall. That is three feet, the size of a big dog. The next size up is a Pony. A Pony is usually less than 58 inches tall. Ponies can be ridden, but Minis cannot. Some Minis are trained to help people with disabilities. They might guide the blind through shopping malls and offices.

Knee-Hi

Knee-Hi at home

Colts and Fillies

Knee-Hi is a colt. That is a young male horse under four years old. A filly is a young female horse of the same age. Foals are baby horses under one year old. Foals can leave their mothers when they are around six months old.

HAPPY

Chapter 6

      Happy's great-grandfather was Seattle Slew, a famous Thoroughbred racehorse. Seattle Slew won the Triple Crown title in 1977. Happy also competed in races and sometimes won.

      Over his first seven years of life, Happy was shuffled from owner to owner. One person paid $40,000 for him! (Most horses cost between a few hundred and a few thousand dollars.) He ended up with an owner who neglected and starved him. Animal Control forced the owner to surrender him to the horse rescue. The workers did not know Happy was a racehorse. Then they found a number tattooed inside his lip. All racehorses are tattooed to identify the horse and its owner.

27

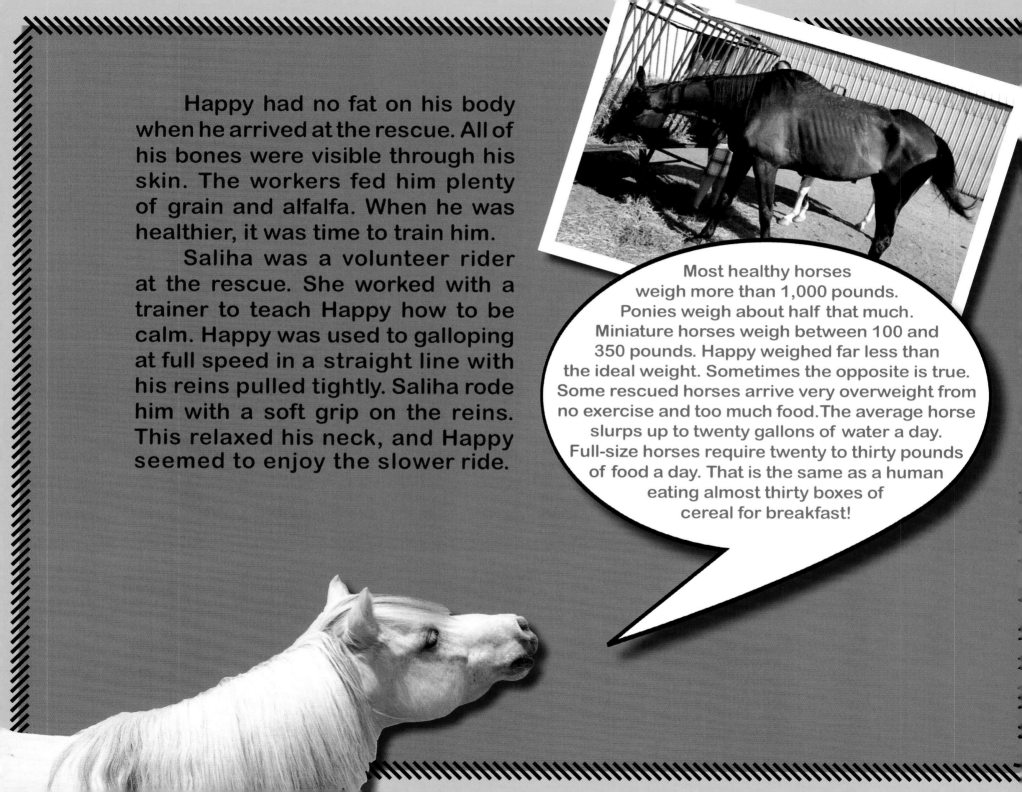

Happy had no fat on his body when he arrived at the rescue. All of his bones were visible through his skin. The workers fed him plenty of grain and alfalfa. When he was healthier, it was time to train him.

Saliha was a volunteer rider at the rescue. She worked with a trainer to teach Happy how to be calm. Happy was used to galloping at full speed in a straight line with his reins pulled tightly. Saliha rode him with a soft grip on the reins. This relaxed his neck, and Happy seemed to enjoy the slower ride.

Most healthy horses weigh more than 1,000 pounds. Ponies weigh about half that much. Miniature horses weigh between 100 and 350 pounds. Happy weighed far less than the ideal weight. Sometimes the opposite is true. Some rescued horses arrive very overweight from no exercise and too much food. The average horse slurps up to twenty gallons of water a day. Full-size horses require twenty to thirty pounds of food a day. That is the same as a human eating almost thirty boxes of cereal for breakfast!

Saliha worked extra hours at her job until she earned enough money to adopt Happy. At the same time, she adopted Smudge to be Happy's companion. Saliha told the rescue workers, "Thanks for making my dreams come true."

The big day arrived for Happy to go to his forever home. The sun dipped behind the Rocky Mountains. Clouds fired up into purple and orange. A truck and trailer rumbled up the long dirt driveway to Saliha's home. The horse rescue workers jumped out. They unloaded Happy and Smudge. Saliha and her family turned the two horses loose into the green pasture with a brand new barn. Tails in the air, the horses took off and played like colts. Happy was happy once again.

Thoroughbreds

Thoroughbreds are bred for the racetrack. The Guinness World Record for the fastest Thoroughbred speed is 43.97 miles per hour. That is as fast as cars go driving around town. There are three important horse races for Thoroughbreds. They are the Kentucky Derby, the Preakness Stakes, and the Belmont Stakes. A horse that wins all three races is called the Triple Crown winner. Only twelve Thoroughbreds have won the Triple Crown in the past 100 years.

The people who work and volunteer at horse rescues give unwanted and unloved horses a better life. They believe all horses deserve to be loved and valued. Rescued horses return that love by being friends and teachers. They also give people hope that things will get better. We can all be thankful there are places for horses to heal and go on to greater things. A place where they are safe at last.

Helping Mistreated Horses

Do you think a horse is being abused? If so, tell a parent or teacher who can contact Animal Control. Animal Control is the part of a city or county government that protects animals. Communities have laws to protect animals from danger. An Animal Control officer will **investigate** to see if an animal law has been broken. Ask an adult to contact Animal Control if you see a horse with these conditions:

- The ribs and hip bones are visible.
- Its hooves are too long. (This makes walking difficult.)
- It has no shelter from the sun or bad weather.
- There is no fresh water available.
- The horse appears to be mistreated.

NEW WORDS

Adopted: to own a horse by paying a fee to a rescue organization.

Blaze: a white stripe on a horse's face.

Disabilities: the condition when a part or parts of the body do not have the ability or power to work well.

Hardy: strong and able to withstand hardships.

Investigate: look into or closely examine.

Malnourished: having too little food or the wrong kinds of food.

Muck: to shovel and remove horse manure.

Nursing: how a mare feeds her baby.

Offspring: a child.

Rescue facility: a place where volunteers and workers care for animals in need.

Scrounged: searched.

Scruffy: ungroomed.

Stockings: the white markings below a horse's knees.

Therapy: helping someone to get better.

Volunteer: a person who offers to help for free.

Whinny: the sound a horse makes. A neigh.

SOURCES

Books:

Alderton, David. *DK Pockets Horses*. New York: DK Publishing, 2003.

Clutton-Brock, Juliet. *DK Eyewitness Horse*. New York: DK Publishing, 2008.

Everts, Tammy, and Bobbie Kalman. *Horses*. New York: Crabtree Pub. Co., 1995.

Havill, Juanita, and Nancy Lane. *Call the Horse Lucky*. Edina, MN: Gryphon Press, 2010.

The Wonder of Horses. San Francisco: Fog City Press, 2013.

Web sites:

livescience.com

en.wikipedia.org/wiki/American_Quarter_Horse

equisearch.com

guinnessworldrecords.com

equine-therapy-programs.com/disabled.html

en.wikipedia.org/wiki/Triple_Crown_of_Thoroughbred_Racing

en.wikipedia.org/wiki/List_of_leading-Thoroughbred-racehorses

Organizations:

Colorado Horse Rescue (where all the rescued horses in this book started their journeys of recovery), 10386 N. 65th St., Longmont, CO 80503, www.chr.org

Steps Foundation (where Topaz now lives and works as a therapy horse), 8590 N. 87th St., Longmont, CO 80503, www.Steps-foundation.org

Wild At Heart (where Jini lives and works as a therapy horse), 10069 N. 65th St., Longmont, CO 80503, www.wildathearttherapy.com/equine-therapy

INDEX

Horse and Animal Rescues

Colorado Horse Rescue: **chr.org**

Denver Dumb Friends League Harmony Equine Center: **ddfl.org**

United States Equine Rescue League, Inc: **userl.org**

Colorado Unwanted Horse Alliance: **counwantedhorse.org**

Denkai Sanctuary: **denkaisanctuary.org**

Homes for Horses Coalition: **homesforhorses.org**

Global Federation of Animal Sanctuaries: **sanctuaryfederation.org/gfas/**

Long Hopes Donkey Shelter: **longhopes.org**

Zuma's Rescue Ranch: **zumasrescueranch.com**

American Society for the Prevention of Cruelty to Animals: **aspca.org**

The Humane Society of the United States: **humanesociety.org.**

Wild Animal Sanctuary: **wildanimalsanctuary.org**

About the Author

Elaine Pease is an award-winning children's author. She lives in Boulder, Colorado. When she's not writing, Elaine enjoys volunteering at Colorado Horse Rescue. Elaine connects her passions—writing and helping horses in need—in *Safe at Last*. She is also the author of *Ghost Over Boulder Creek*, *Tallie's Christmas Lights Surprise*, *Even Sharks Need Friends*, and *I'll Never Leave*.

Elaine welcomes comments from her readers. Email her at ryspease@yahoo.com. For information on inviting Elaine to your classroom or library, please visit peasepodbooks.com.

About the Photographer

Roxanne Capaul is CHR's Creative Director. She came to Colorado in 1990 from Washington State. She has worked with Colorado Horse Rescue for the last seven years.

Her passion for animals and creative skills combine to make for a great life experience and one that she will always cherish.